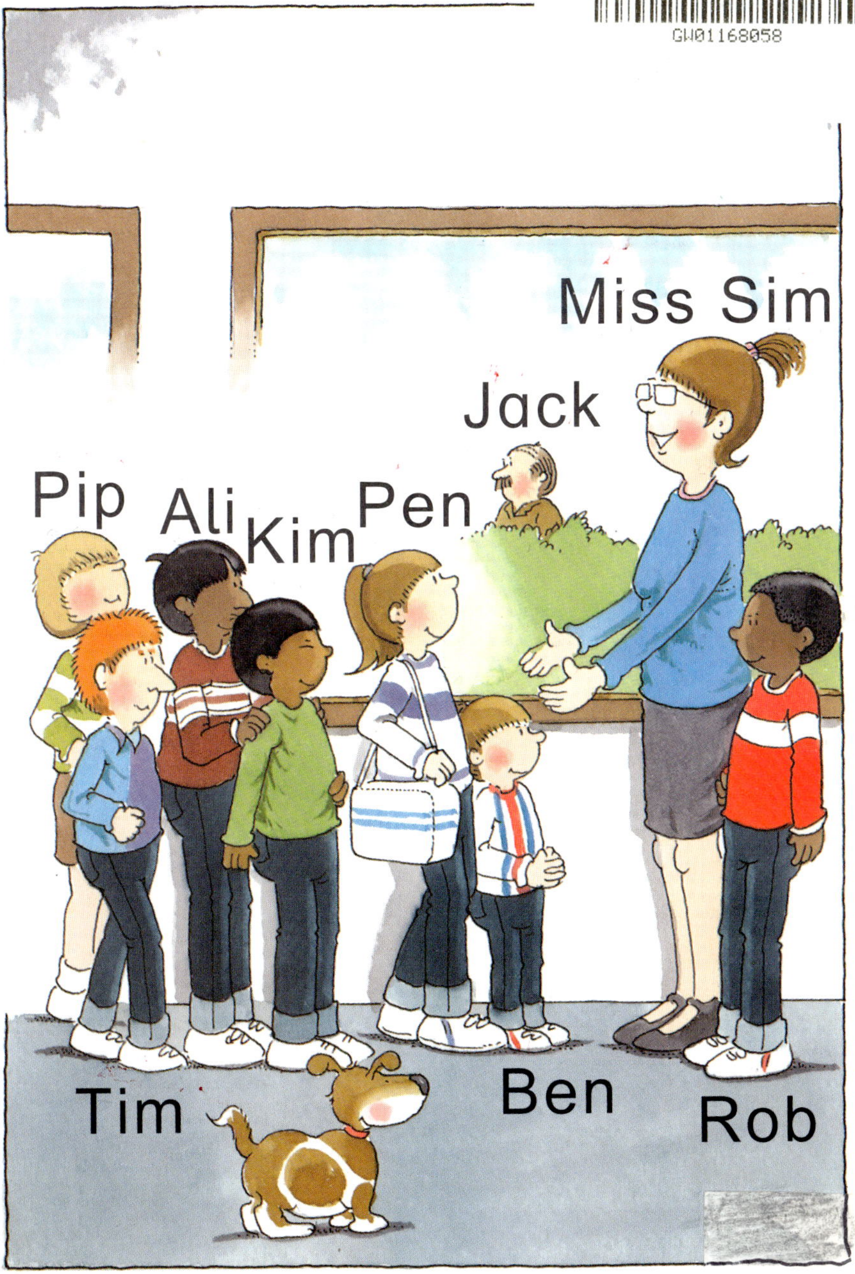
Miss Sim
Jack
Pip
Ali
Kim
Pen
Tim
Ben
Rob

We like Miss Sim.

Miss Sim

Pen

Ben

Pip

Rob

4

We like to help Miss Sim.

Ali helps Miss Sim.

Tim helps Miss Sim.

Ali and Tim
help Miss Sim.

7

Pip helps Miss Sim.

Rob helps Miss Sim.

Rob and Pip help Miss Sim.

Pen and Ben and Tim help Miss Sim.

We like Miss Sim.
We like to help Miss Sim.

Jack likes to help Miss Sim.
Miss Sim likes Jack to help!